BLACK SHEEP
Kick Azz!

BLACK SHEEP
Kick Azz!

10 Kick Azz Principles
for fed up employees ready to discover,
protect and pursue their unique
God- given purposes!

Aku Esther Oparah

Library of Congress Control Number:		2016903821
ISBN:	Hardcover	978-1-5144-7375-7
	Softcover	978-1-5144-7374-0
	eBook	978-1-5144-7373-3

Print information available on the last page.

Rev. date: 03/30/2016

To order additional copies of this book, contact:
Xlibris
1-888-795-4274
www.Xlibris.com
Orders@Xlibris.com
732448

CONTENTS

Acknowledgments vii

Dedication ix

The Promise xi

Principle "B" Believe In Your Black Sheep Spirit 1

Principle "L" Love The Details And Clarify Your Purpose 6

Principle "A" All Is Forgiven...I Am Where Am 10

Principle "C" Clarity Through Contrast 14

Principle "K" Kick Attraction In The Azz! 19

Principle "S" Seeing Is Not Believing 32

Principle "H" The Herd 38

Principle "E¹" Easy Does It But Make Sure You Do It! 45

Principle "E²" Expect Abundance 52

Principle "P" Praise Your Progress 59

About the Author 67

NOTES

ACKNOWLEDGMENTS

First and foremost, I would like to thank GOD for blessing me with this journey. For many years, I felt that God was holding my life's purpose captive and would not reveal it to me. After years of studying personal development and transforming my mind-set, I now understand that my life's purpose is to feel joy, love, passion, and freedom *through serving humanity,* all of which are attributes of God. I can never go wrong with good intentions, and my job is to continue to walk through life with an expectation that ALL will work out in my favor.

I would also like to thank God for moments that do NOT feel good. It is through these experiences that I gain clarity of what I DO desire. This remarkable emotional guidance system that God has created in all of us acts as an indicator of the strength of my connection to Good—to God. I've realized the **work** is to **first become aware** of any negative thoughts and then **replace** those negative thoughts with statements that feel better or affirmations of love and gratitude.

Second, I would like to thank my family. Thank you Ma and Doddy for believing in me from the day I was born. Your silent yet consistent support allowed me the **freedom** to walk my own path as an adult and discover who Aku REALLY was and not who you wanted me to be. I acknowledge the good intentions behind your guidance. I thank my brothers for also believing in their little sister and silently allowing me to reveal my Divine Self to the world.

Next, I would like to thank my beautiful and precious daughter, Anaya Chizoma. The joy I feel nurturing you is what has motivated me to keep pursuing my dream of a life of joy, freedom, and purpose. I will always encourage you to follow your bliss and pursue that which brings you joy—and **never** allow judgment from other people to deter you from your destiny. You are an extension of God, Pure Love, and

Joy—**living your bliss is your God-given right.** "Who loves you the *most*?" That's right, baby girl—God. ☺

Last but not least, I would like to thank my friends, especially Reese who has shown me what love and patience can REALLY do for a friendship. Thank you for always being the first to support me, take care of me, and stand by my side through ALL kinds of weather. No one but God knows me better than you! You have taught me that TRUE love forgives, sticks around, and never gives up! More importantly, God could not have provided a better father for our daughter. ☺

DEDICATION

I would like to dedicate this workshop to my friends who believed in me and in themselves in the first Mastermind group I ever started. It is because of our experience that this guide was born. So I thank you, Reese, Dyann, Yvette, Zandra, Sharina, and Danny. I love you all. ☺

NOTES

THE PROMISE

Prepare to mentally and spiritually commit to find and pursue your passion despite judgment from yourself or from other people.

- Do you work a full-time job that is stressing you out?
- Do you feel depressed on Sundays or whenever you anticipate going back to work?
- Do you feel like you have a higher purpose in life but have no idea where to start or how to start?
- Have you shared a dream business with those close to you only to get a bunch negative feedback?
- Do you feel overwhelmed from the expectation of work and family obligations?
- Do you feel invisible, underappreciated, or undercompensated at your workplace?
- Do you look around your workplace and notice constant complaining from coworkers who are too fearful to find another job? Are you one of the complainers?
- Do you spend time at work surfing the internet yearning to find your passion?
- Have you become physically ill from the stress of your work activities?
- Are you short-tempered with your family, friends, and coworkers?
- Do you feel resentment or jealousy toward others that have pursued their passion and are experiencing a life of wealth, purpose, and bliss?
- Are you abusing drugs and alcohol to mask the stress of work?
- Have you gained or lost a significant amount of weight due to stress?

If you answered YES to any of the questions above, you may be stressed the hell out, and certainly you are NOT alone! Over 70 percent of Americans are unhappy at their jobs. Guess why? The no. 1 reason people are unhappy at their jobs is because they feel a lack of appreciation. These companies are now on a mission to give two or three jobs to one employee. They are exploiting salaried employees by forcing them to work extended hours for a forty-hour-a-week pay. They are exploiting hourly employees by forcing them to perform more activities with no pay increase. As a result, you sacrifice those once-in-a-lifetime events with your family. You are always exhausted, and when you finally get a day off, you THINK you will move the heavens and make up for lost time. But because your body will eventually get the rest it needs, you find yourself passed out from exhaustion only to wake up to go right back to work!

You deserve to live the life that was uniquely and divinely designed for you by God. Your potential must not be determined by those who are afraid or have failed at fulfilling their own passions. Every morning you open your eyes is God's way of approving another opportunity to start over and make the commitment to be more of who you were destined to become. The BSKA Principles will help you gain the strength to step up and stand up for your passion. The result after completing this guide? Relief from stress at the job and a life of joy, purpose, passion, and FREEDOM!

> God's gift to you was LIFE. The way you live your life
> is your gift to God. (Anonymous)

My name is **Aku Esther Oparah,** and I created this guide after years of waking up to go to a job I knew and felt in my gut was not my passion. I was twenty-seven years old when I began wondering about the rest of my life. I was surrounded by shitty coworkers who chose to show up every day and complain. I felt so alone in a whirlwind of frustration as I forced myself to smile at people that admired my salary and position. No one could really understand the depth of burnout I experienced. I didn't even understand what I was experiencing. I just knew I was making a good salary and I was NOT HAPPY!

What changed my life was attending a seminar where I heard a motivational speaker for the first time. His name was Les Brown. My soul shook as I listened to this man speak to my spirit as he gave it validation and power! He said the following words that would become my spiritual rod and staff: *"Whatever you're seeking is also seeking you."*

It was then that I began to ask God questions about my passion, my life's purpose, and the meaning of life. Eventually, I received the answers to all of my questions and more! See, I had to make a COMMITMENT that I would discover what was possible for me. Once I made the commitment to discover my purpose, new information began to appear in my awareness. The more I became aware that this new information was God's answers to my questions, the clearer I began to see the pathway to my destiny. I continued to take action, and what I found after exploring and researching for over ten-plus years were principles that took me from crying in the company parking lot to living a life of PURPOSE! The problem is that most of you can't or won't commit to discover your potential. Most people have become complacent with feeling like shit! Many people wake up every day expecting to feel like shit then they go to shitty jobs, surround themselves with the "shitty committee," then wonder why their day is so shitty!

Most people won't pursue their passions because they can't stomach the possibility of looking embarrassed in front of their family and friends. Other people's opinions of the way we live our lives have crippled so many magnificent goals and dreams. Our family and friends may have convinced us that we have only ONE shot at greatness. Some secretly have their "I Told You So!" poster boards and flags ready and waiting for us to fail.

There are a few programs or systems that offer a roadmap to prepare you for this type of journey. I visited about a dozen churches desperately trying to find a spiritual path. I would attend service on Sunday, but by Tuesday, I was back to feeling depressed, angry, and stuck until the following Sunday. We ALL know people that attend services regularly. Can you honestly say the majority of the people you know that attend church regularly are living the life of their dreams? Or are they going through life thanking God for the good things that happen then saving up all their obstacles and mistakes until Sunday to blame the "devil"? There are LESSONS in those "obstacles and mistakes" that must be acknowledged in order to GROW from them and prepare you for the next obstacle or mistake. People have been conditioned to blame an OUTSIDE source as if they had no part in adverse events that happens to EVERYONE at some point in our lives.

The BLACK SHEEP Kick-Azz Principles are designed to maintain your Sunday morning "MOJO" so to speak. These ten principles will sustain that "after-church service" spiritual charge that leaves us feeling so good and ready to take action to pursue our dreams.

Once I decided that life had more to offer than waking up every day to compromise my integrity, I made the COMMITMENT to discover my passion. Once I incorporated these ten principles, my life was transformed.

- I felt motivated and excited to seek my higher purpose despite the opinions of others.
- My negative thought patterns were replaced with positive thoughts surrounding my passion and dreams.
- I noticed my burnout symptoms slowly disappear.
- I found it easier and easier to deal with my work activities and shitty coworkers.
- I felt empowered to give my passion a backbone and created a vision of my dreams.
- I was relieved to discover so many people with the same dilemma and even more relieved to know there was a solution.
- I joined an unbiased group designed to support and hold me accountable to achieve my dreams so I will not live a life of regrets.
- I felt inspired to learn how spiritual laws applied to my life and assisted me in reprogramming my thought patterns.
- I became aware of the voices and disguises of the "Herd" and how those voices affected my progress.
- I let go of any resentment or jealous feelings of others who were pursuing their passion or had achieved their goals.

After ten years of prolonged stress, I found myself walking out the doors of a pharmaceutical company. It was my last day as a Project Manager. I was fired from a job for the first time in my life. Well, they fired me, but I had already mentally quit my first day there! My mind said to feel humiliated. My mind said to not tell anyone so they wouldn't grab their poster boards and flags. My mind wanted me to shrink and disappear. But my BLACK SHEEP spirit knew it was really the first day of the rest of my life! My BLACK SHEEP spirit knew that God made NO mistakes. My spirit knew that I was finally released from the prison of my mind and I was now free to live the life of the mother, sister, friend, and teacher that I was destined to become! I went on a quest to find a supportive group of like-minded people that were tired of living a passionless life and were instead pursuing their dreams. When I could only find "get rich quick" type groups, I decided to start my own with a group of friends that all were tired of feeling stressed and wanted to pursue their passions. Although the energy was high at the first couple of meetings, as the meetings continued, member after member began to drop out. The group ended after about seven meetings.

I was disappointed, but I knew that there was a great lesson to be learned. I discovered the reason the Master Mind group was so short-lived. It was short-lived because I was the only one that had made a *quantum* leap in my mental and spiritual transition. I was ten-plus years into my spiritual journey and ready to hold myself accountable. I unknowingly was asking my friends to hold themselves accountable to goals *they never conditioned themselves to believe in!* They had not made the COMMITMENT to discover their potential.

See, once you make the COMMITMENT, your reasons "why," which come from the unique BLACK SHEEP spirit of who you are, grow and expand. Your drive to achieve increases, which focuses and increases the energy you emit. You will begin to experience opportunities and events that support your COMMITTMENT. A support group is essential to help get over the obstacles you WILL encounter. This is called LIFE full of obstacles and triumphs, which are BOTH opportunities for GROWTH.

Everything on this planet grows. If you are not growing, you are dying. (Tony Robbins)

The following year, I decided to create the BLACK SHEEP Kick-Azz Principles to prepare anyone to become spiritually and mentally committed to discovering and pursuing their passion despite the opinion of others. It is designed as a tool to empower millions of burned-out workers to make a decision to stay or to transition from their current jobs to pursue their passions. Either decision will be inspired and empowered from your unique BLACK SHEEP Spirit!

These principles are the result of my experience with the difficulty of leaving "comfortable discomfort" to discover and pursue my destiny. My objective is for you to wake up in the morning excited about the day, feeling ALIVE with PURPOSE and PASSION. You will feel significant again as a mother, sister, wife, employee, or entrepreneur! Isn't living a life with purpose and passion what life is all about? Why NOT you? I only wish a guide like this was available to me during my years of burnout. If it was, I would have made an easier and more strategic transition from my job. Instead, I ran out the door and nearly started to break-dance in the parking lot without any real plan of what to do or where to go—it still felt great. ☺

When you FEEL like you are living your life with purpose and with passion, there is no longer room to FEEL burned out. Those symptoms of feeling unmotivated, unappreciated, angry, short-tempered, and exhausted will be experienced at a minimal level or not at all. You will become too busy FEELING happy and excited about your new life and your new journey.

So whether you choose to stay or leave, you will encounter feedback from yourself and others that you MUST be able to withstand.

For example, if you choose to stay at your current job, you may have to deal with disgruntled coworkers ("shitty committee") that are too scared to find another job. You may have to deal with an insecure boss who underappreciates you or the company policies that continue to take away your benefits. You will absolutely need to change your thought patterns toward the traffic woes of your daily commute and the stress of not spending as much time with your family, all of which will continue to cause physical and mental damage if you are not spiritually prepared to cope.

On the other hand, if you choose to transition and pursue your passion, you MUST be prepared to handle other forms of feedback. Some or all of your friends and family may think you're crazy and constantly try to talk you out of it. You may even find some "friends" drop off from your life. You may tell yourself you're crazy for thinking about leaving. Television news programs do a fantastic job at programming negativity about the world and the economy. They have successfully made society think that the government, banks, and different races of people are the cause of our positions in life.

Either way, these BLACK SHEEP Kick-Azz Principles will enforce your spiritual backbone to make the decision to live your life with purpose; and as a result, the burnout symptoms will significantly decrease or disappear completely.

> You don't get what you think about; you get how you
> FEEL about what you think about. (Aku)

We all come to a point in our lives when we begin to think about our higher purpose in life. We begin to make mental notations of things we want to accomplish in life. We assume that our life purpose will one day fall into our lap. The truth is, our purpose has been reaching out to us all along! Those faint voices you hear when you see a commercial for an invention that you thought of years ago or the FEELING you get when you look at that sewing machine you haven't used in years—these are all methods your spirit uses to communicate to you where your passions lie.

Your spirit communicates to you using what Abraham-Hicks in *Ask and It Is Given* calls "emotional guidance." How do you know your life's purpose? It's the butterflies in your stomach when you notice that certain tool or gadget that you've always wanted on sale or get a big idea about a business you want to start. It's that nervousness you feel when you begin to think about what's POSSIBLE for you. It's that surge of energy you feel holding a Powerball ticket minutes before the drawing. Your whole life flashes before your eyes while your heart rate increases and you smile at the anticipation of fulfilling all of your life's desires.

The only thing that matters is the way you FEEL. Dr. Wayne Dyer says, "When we FEEL good, we FEEL God." I believe there is only one God or one Source. God IS All-Good, Pure Love, Well-Being, and All-Giving. God created us in His image, so we are an extension of God, of Good, of Pure Love, of Well-Being, and All-Giving. When we feel Good, we are connecting to God at the highest level on an emotional scale.

When you FEEL bad, you are moving further away from God lowering your energy level. Since God is Pure Love and there is only one God, one Source, can evil exist? I believe NO. Evil is a state of SPIRIT. Many people interpret evil as an "outside" force that takes control. Some people have even assigned "evil" a skin tone! What most call evil or the devil is actually a frayed connection to Good—to God. If anyone of these so-called "evil" people were removed from their environment and were fed positive feedback about their potential rather than their limitations, they will slowly begin to FEEL better. Their energy level will rise along with the way they FEEL about themselves, moving them up the emotional guidance scale to connect with God, Good, Pure Love, Well-Being, and All-Giving at the highest level.

So let us start this journey together and begin to peel back some layers so you can reveal to yourself and to the world who you really are. Keep in mind that **wherever you are right now is perfectly okay**. You are NOT ALONE by any means. Get excited and congratulate yourself for stepping up and giving destiny a chance! The BLACK SHEEP in you (your authentic self, your unique God-given SPIRIT) HAS LED YOU HERE and will continue to guide you to all of your dreams and desires.

The BLACK SHEEP KICK-AZZ Principles are ten principles I've learned from several of my virtual friends including but not limited to Les Brown, Oprah Winfrey, Dr. Wayne Dyer, Kevin Trudeau, Lisa Nichols, Bob Proctor, Abraham-Hicks, Tony Robbins, Jack Canfield, Napoleon Hill, Brendon Burchard, and Christy Whitman. Each letter in B.L.A.C.K. S.H.E.E.P. describes a principle and includes journaling exercises to ensure that you are properly applying the principles in your daily activities.

The ten principles covered in the B.L.A.C.K. S.H.E.E.P. Kick-Azz guide are as follows:

1. **Principle "B"—BELIEVE IN YOUR BLACK SHEEP**

   The BLACK SHEEP is the part of you that is not defined by the opinions of society or the ego. A BLACK SHEEP lives a life of passion and purpose, is nonjudgmental, and is satisfied with where it is with excited anticipation of blessings to come. Explore the blissful lifestyle of a BLACK SHEEP that embraces and protects its **unique** God-given purpose and talents.

2. **Principle "L"—LOVE THE DETAILS ... CLARIFY YOUR PURPOSE**

   Learn how to become clear and specific about your purpose and create a compelling crystal-clear vision by completing these exercises. Then finish by writing your own heartfelt personal mission statement. The more detailed your intention, the more confidence you'll gain to **BELIEVE** that you will achieve your goals.

3. **Principle "A"—ALL IS FORGIVEN ... I AM WHERE I AM**

   You will learn how to forgive the decisions you've made in the past as well as the decisions others have made that **you've allowed to affect your life.** You are where you are based on decisions **only you have made.** Learn how to **own it and start a new set point from LOVE.**

4. **Principle "C"—<u>C</u>LARITY THROUGH CONTRAST**

We all know what we DON'T want. You will discover what you DO want with even more clarity by completing this process. You will feel **relief** once you identify the key contributors to your burnout symptoms and create a desire statement with affirmations describing the way you **want to feel**.

5. **Principle "K"—<u>K</u>ICK ATTRACTION IN THE AZZ!**

You can't hear the music of your life's purpose over all that background noise! I've listed eight of the fastest and most powerful ways to connect to your unique Divine Self, your BLACK SHEEP spirit. One way listed is through practicing meditation. Learn how to meditate, a perfect lesson for beginners.

6. **Principle "S"—<u>S</u>EEING IS NOT BELIEVING . . . <u>B</u>ELIEVING IS SEEING**

You've watched hundreds of movie directors use their passion to bring their visions to life. You will learn how to be the director of your dream life with this scripting and visioning exercise! You will **feel empowered to give your passion a backbone** as you create a vision to believe in your dreams.

7. **Principle "H" — The <u>H</u>ERD**

The "HERD" is an all-encompassing group of voices that represents your ego, past experiences, your conscious, the influence of other people and the subliminal messages from negative TV programs. The HERD will lead you to your fears; your **heart** will lead you to your passion.

8. **Principle "E¹"—EASY DOES IT . . . BUT MAKE SURE YOU DO IT!**

   Written goals are a BLACK SHEEP's purpose, dreams, and desires confidently projected to the universe with targets and deadlines. Learn the best way to write your goals with sustained motivation and how to manage your time more effectively.

9. **Principle "E²"—EXPECT ABUNDANCE!**

   The amount of abundance you attract is in direct proportion to the clarity and intensity of your vision, faith, and gratitude. You will discover if you are living in a **spiritual state of lack** and what steps to take to live a life that attracts abundance.

10. **Principle "P"—PRAISE YOUR PROGRESS**

    You will learn the importance of **appreciating where you are right now**. Feel a sense of **ultimate gratitude** as you complete exercises that will leave you feeling optimistic, empowered, and centered. Remember, you will never truly arrive at your destiny because you will always have a desire to grow—**the joy is in the journey**!

The BSKA Principles are **NOT** ideal for those who want to fit in and remain comfortable. These principles are **ONLY** for those who want to stand out as one of the few that dared to dream for a life full of purpose and joy. I transitioned the hard way, and I want to show you the easier and faster way. The BSKA Principles are for you if you feel deep inside that you have not served your higher purpose with the work you are currently doing. You can live a purpose-filled life while still working your full-time job!

I understand the frustration of feeling overworked and underappreciated. I woke up to sit in traffic two to four hours a day!

I understand the frustration of never getting a chance to chaperone field trips and missing school plays and assemblies. I only slept three to four hours stressed out every night, and I only spent time with my daughter on weekends!

Most of you have passions and talents that remain untouched because of fear. It does not have to be that way. You simply need to reprogram your thought patterns and learn how to become AWARE of the HERD's voices and disguises. The burnout symptoms that you are experiencing are red flags from your spirit telling you your thoughts and God's calling for you are out of sync.

I knew there was something more I was meant to do, but it wasn't easy to find with so many voices telling me what I **COULD NOT DO**. So I took a huge risk to get my time and freedom back, and I did it the hard and expensive way. You can take it slow and steady.

So **STOP** wasting energy gossiping about entertainers on television that are living THEIR passion. Instead, use that time to become the reality star of your own life! Allow your light to guide your children, family, and friends to also step out and pursue their own passions despite the opinion of others!

There are NO ACCIDENTS. If you are still reading this, your higher purpose is trying to communicate to you and has brought you a resource to help you achieve your dreams.

Will today be the day you START?

I recommend the following as you complete this guide:

- Although there is ample space to complete the exercises, I recommend you acquire a journal to write down any additional thoughts and profound revelations.
- Please complete each exercise before advancing to the next. Your initial response is your most unbiased response.

🐑 Take note of any additional questions and/or concerns and feel free to e-mail me at <u>Aku@blacksheepkickazz.com.</u>

So let's get started to discover the BLACK SHEEP in you!

NOTES

PRINCIPLE "B"

"BELIEVE IN THE 'BLACK
SHEEP' IN YOU!"

The "BLACK SHEEP" SPIRIT is
the part of you that is not defined by
the opinions of society or the ego. Your
BLACK SHEEP lives a life of passion
and purpose, is non-judgmental and is
satisfied with where it is with excited
anticipation of blessings to come.

The name "BLACK SHEEP KICK AZZ" comes from my celebration and admiration to all who live by the uniqueness of their soul. The name is a tribute to those who freely express themselves without fear of judgment. We are ALL BLACK SHEEP spirits because no two people are exactly alike. Each one of us has unique talents and abilities that exemplify our spiritual potential, but too few us have the gonads to actually do it!

Living by your BLACK SHEEP spirit is by no means EASY. In life and at work, it is a consistent effort to avoid toxic energy, especially because the shitty committee, society, and mainstream media are on a mission to make us feel like we SHOULD be separate. After decades of being brainwashed in this manner, most people's BLACK SHEEP spirits have taken a seat at the back of their minds, leaving them fearful to step up and stand out.

Your Black Sheep Spirit kicks azz when you are **always** aware of the way you **feel and WHY.** It's when you're at work or home and you know without a doubt that the only thing that matters is that you **FEEL GOOD ABOUT WHO YOU ARE.** When you **FEEL GOOD,** you **FEEL GOD.** In feeling God, the BLACK SHEEP in you is unafraid to express its unique authentic self. It uses your God-given talents as its purpose to serve humanity. It will step up and stand out from the back of your mind, claiming its rightful position at the forefront of your mind, body, and soul. It will lead you to discover your passion while granting you freedom in an adventurous journey as you experience living a life of joy and bliss.

But FIRST, you must make the COMMITMENT to discover your potential. You must know WHY it's important that you live a life at your highest potential. Who or what will be affected by your achievements? Your family? Your spouse? Your finances? Your children's futures?

What is YOUR commitment to God?

I will commit to . . .

_____

_____

_____

so that I can enjoy . . .

_____

_____

_____

I WILL commit to my commitment because . . .

_____

_____

_____

The BLACK SHEEP in you realizes that its perspective is uncommon so a supportive environment is absolutely **critical** in maintaining its motivation to persevere. When your BLACK SHEEP spirit actively seeks to be surrounded by like-minded individuals, as spiritual law applies, it will attract other like-minded BLACK SHEEP spirits.

The *BLACK SHEEP KICK AZZ Online Course Program* includes admission to a private group forum comprised of like-minded people like you with a passion to protect, pursue, and celebrate their passions!

A BLACK SHEEP understands that **continuous education** allows it to grow so it willingly invests in materials that enhance its intellect and spiritual muscle. (I've gained my knowledge from the many programs, seminars, and workshops I've invested in, and I'm always nervous with both knees shaking!)

A BLACK SHEEP immediately recognizes the disguises of the HERD (see Principle "H"). It respects and accepts the HERD as a part of you. A BLACK SHEEP knows that the HERD's true intention by **genetic design** is to keep you safe from harm, which oftentimes results in keeping you in FEAR. A BLACK SHEEP *will hear what the HERD has to say* then kindly respond, "Thanks for the feedback, but no thanks."

Your BLACK SHEEP spirit is ALWAYS loving, kind, and treats others as it would want to be treated. It understands that the energy and feelings it emits into the universe will manifest itself as circumstances and encounters in the physical world.

Your BLACK SHEEP spirit does NOT feel the need to judge. It understands that those that judge are insecure about the very things they pass judgment about in others. A BLACK SHEEP recognizes that one's circumstances could always be worse or better; therefore passing judgment is futile, and it lowers your energy on an emotional scale.

A BLACK SHEEP spirit in the workplace accepts and respects everyone despite their shitty behavior. It recognizes that everyone has their own history that has shaped who they've become. No one's actions will sway a BLACK SHEEP's spirit; they will succeed with or without you!

Principle "B" Reflection

1. What feelings arose after reading about the life of a BLACK SHEEP?

_____

_____

_____

_____

_____

2. What questions arose?

_____

_____

_____

_____

_____

3. In what ways do you recognize your BLACK SHEEP spirit?

_____

_____

_____

_____

_____

PRINCIPLE "L"

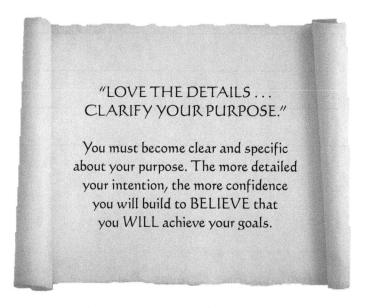

"LOVE THE DETAILS ...
CLARIFY YOUR PURPOSE."

You must become clear and specific
about your purpose. The more detailed
your intention, the more confidence
you will build to BELIEVE that
you WILL achieve your goals.

Life Purpose Statement (portions from Jack Canfield's *Success Principles*)

Finding your purpose is really discovering what you were put on this Earth to do. Your purpose can tell you what to accomplish, for whom, how to accomplish. When you discover your purpose, life flows effortlessly. Opportunities seem to fall in your lap. Resources and relationships find you easily. Small successes build upon one another to create an unstoppable momentum.

But how does purpose differ from goals or action plans?

Purpose is the "why"—the reason you create the goals you create and pursue the activities you do. It's the reason you strive to achieve the results you're looking for.

Goals are merely the "what" you'll accomplish and action plans are simply the "how" you'll accomplish those goals.

Without PURPOSE as the compass, goals and action plans are meaningless.

Every living creature on earth has a God-given purpose. I believe our purpose as human beings is to find the way we best **serve others**.

To determine your life's purpose—to develop it in crystal-clear words that are compelling to you and others—take time now to complete the exercises that follow. Then finish by writing your own heartfelt personal mission statement.

Today's Date: _____

1. List two of your unique personal qualities. If you have difficulty, think of compliments you've received from others or strengths that have been identified by management.

(For example, are you enthusiastic, creative, personable, organized, etc.?)

_____

_____

2. List one or two ways you enjoy expressing those qualities when interacting with others.

(For example, do you show enthusiasm to raise morale? Are you creative to inspire? Are you personable to bring joy? Are you organized to ease chaos?)

_____

_____

_____

_____

_____

3. Assume that the world is perfect right now. What does the world look like? How is everyone interacting with everyone else? How are you serving humanity? What does it **feel** like? This is a statement, in present tense, describing the ultimate condition, the perfect world as you see it and **feel** it. Remember that a perfect world is a fun place to be.

(*For example, everyone is freely expressing their own unique talents. Everyone is working in harmony. Everyone is expressing love. I serve others by teaching self-expression.*)

_____

_____

_____

_____

_____

_____

_____

_____

4. Combine the three responses above into a single statement.

(For example, my purpose is to use my creativity and enthusiasm to support and inspire others to freely express their talents in a harmonious and loving way)

My purpose is to . . .

_____

_____

_____

_____

_____

_____

_____

_____

5. How do you feel after writing your purpose statement?

_____

_____

_____

_____

PRINCIPLE "A"

> ### "ALL IS FORGIVEN . . . I AM WHERE I AM."
>
> You must forgive the decisions you've made in the past as well as the decisions others have made that you've allowed to affect your life. You are where you are based on decisions only you made. Own it. Start a new set point from love . . . GOOD, now let's move on!

Your BLACK SHEEP is always aware of its emotional set point. It's able to quickly reconnect to its Divine Purpose and is okay whether someone says they are sorry or not.

There are no perfect human beings. We are all a product of our environment. Every single person carries with them all the negative and positive feedback we've received from our environment since birth. The mistake we make is in the expectation that everyone we come in contact with will behave in a way that keeps us happy. This assumption that everyone should hold our happiness as a priority is just not practical.

When we wait for other people's behavior to change before we can feel happiness, we are projecting to the universe a feeling of "not enough." As a result, our obedient universe will manifest more experiences to confirm the feeling that your BLACK SHEEP, your Divine Self, is "not enough." Spiritual laws are at work whether we like it or not!

Remember . . .

*"Hurt people . . . **hurt** people."*

We react shocked, angry, and blindsided when someone in our lives makes a decision that benefits THEM but hurts **OUR** feelings. It is at that precise moment that we CHOOSE how their decision will affect our path to joy, purpose, and freedom.

One of the main reasons I chose to remain in a passionless profession was because of the continuous anger and blame I felt throughout my day. I felt like a victim and that I deserved the misery and frustration I was experiencing. I walked around all day blaming everybody else for MY situation. I blamed my parents for brainwashing me into believing I wanted to be a doctor. I blamed my high school and college guidance counselors for not identifying my talents, skills, and strengths. I even blamed ex-boyfriends for wasting years of my life on them when I could have done more with my education. I found it very difficult to hold myself accountable. I was stuck in this world of resentment, and I felt that all my blaming **was justified**.

I learned from Dr. Wayne Dyer that there are no "justified resentments." I learned that the anger, hatred, and revenge that we hold in our bodies act as a poison in our veins. It is imperative that you let that resentment go from your body and allow love and peace to enter. When you are constantly reminding yourself that you've been wronged, you are projecting a "I'm a victim" **feeling** and vibration to the universe, and as spiritual law applies itself, the universe will manifest more circumstances and experiences that confirm your "I am a victim" **feeling** or vibration. Many times prolonged resentment manifests into emotional or even physical abuse of yourself, your spouse, your coworkers, or your children. The HERD's negative thoughts have settled into our subconscious, and it does NOT want us to change or to move on. A certain level of comfort has been established in that deep-seated hate and anger because it has become a way of life for many people. As Les Brown says, "Let go . . . or be dragged." You will continue to unconsciously drag that emotional baggage into every facet of your life, blaming the world and never taking ownership for your own decisions.

It's not easy to forgive and hold yourself accountable. Forgiveness does not happen automatically. It's a conscious effort that must be repeated on a daily basis. You would have achieved true forgiveness at the moment you stop feeling hatred, anger, or resentment when you think about that person or that particular event in your life.

Complete the following questions and revert to them on a daily basis until you are able to **choose kindness over being "right."** You may want to journal your responses if you need extra space.

> Forgiveness is the fragrance that the violet sheds on the heel that has crushed it. (Mark Twain)

Principle "A" Reflection

1. What decisions have **you** made that require your forgiveness?

_____

_____

_____

_____

_____

2. If you **don't** forgive the person, people, or event that affected your life, how will you continue to feel?

_____

_____

_____

_____

_____

3. If you **do** forgive the person, people, or event that affected your life, how will you feel? How will releasing the blame affect your life?

_____

_____

_____

_____

4. What action steps can you take to begin to heal and choose kindness over being "right"?

_____

_____

_____

_____

PRINCIPLE "C"

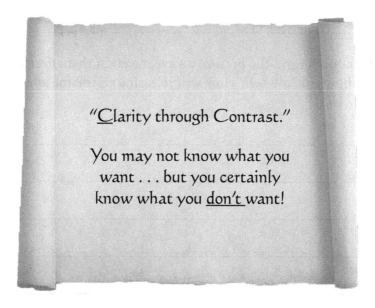

"Clarity through Contrast."

You may not know what you want . . . but you certainly know what you don't want!

"Clarity through Contrast" is one of my favorite processes I learned during my life coach certification process from Christy Whitman at the Quantum Success Coaching Academy. This process helped me understand with better clarity my preferred desires and purpose. The negative feelings (the "contrast") I experienced from my last job caused me to become aware of what I actually did want ("the clarity"). After completing this process, I felt more confident about my intentions, and I felt more focused toward the achievement of my dreams and desires.

Your negative (contrast) experiences should be used as an indicator to clarify your purpose and divine desires. This is not an easy task. We have been mentally and spiritually programmed to become aware of our limitations for most of our lives. To recognize and shift our "stinkin' thinkin'" takes practice over time.

On the next page, you will notice two columns. On the left side under "Contrast," list all the things that you are unhappy about regarding your career choice, workplace environment, scheduling, compensation, life purpose, etc.

After you've completed the "Contrast" side, read back each entry on your list now, asking yourself, "**What do I want instead?**" As you answer each entry, cross it out under "Contrast" and write what you do want under "Clarity." As you write each entry under "Clarity," notice how your emotional set point raises as you imagine experiencing these clarifying statements.

Contrast	Clarity

Next, on the following page, write a "Desire Statement" to further clarify your intention by writing as if what you want has already happened for you. Writing this statement will get you into the "feeling" place of your dreams come true. Within the body, you will use the "Clarity" statements you listed in the previous activity. Write the "Body" in the "Desire Statement" in the space provided or in your journal if you need more space.

🐏 Write this **Opening Statement**:

"I am in the process of attracting all that I need to be, do, know, and have to attract my ideal desire."

🐏 Next, write the **Body:**

Write out the body using your "**Clarity**" statements from the previous exercise. You may start off the body using phrases like "I love knowing that my ideal . . .," "I love how it feels when . . .," "I've decided . . .," "It excites me that . . .," "Thank you God for blessing me with . . .," "I feel joyful because . . ."; then end each phrase with one of your clarity statements.

🐏 Finally, write this **Closing Statement**:

"God is unfolding and orchestrating all that needs to happen to bring me my desire."

Desire Statement

_____

_____

_____

_____

_____

_____

_____

_____

_____

_____

_____

_____

_____

_____

_____

_____

_____

Read your Desire Statement aloud. Record your feelings below.

_____

_____

_____

_____

_____

_____

_____

_____

_____

_____

_____

_____

_____

_____

_____

PRINCIPLE "K"

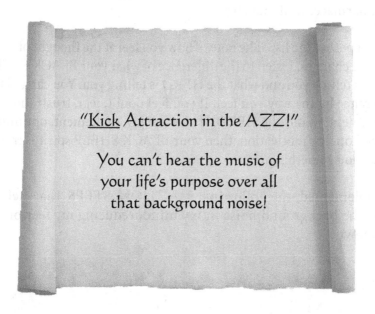

"<u>Kick</u> Attraction in the AZZ!"

You can't hear the music of
your life's purpose over all
that background noise!

The following simple changes allowed me to hear my higher calling louder and clearer. Remember, we are **spiritual beings created by God** housed in physical bodies. God is Pure Love, Well-Being, and All-Giving. Therefore, we are an extension of God and of Pure Love, Well-Being, and All-Giving. I've listed all the simple lifestyle changes I've implemented over the years. I advise you to implement them one at a time, each for twenty-one days.

Be sure to journal your successes for each and especially pay attention to how you **feel,** and journal those feelings as well. If you can implement all of these changes for a trial of twenty-one days, then brace yourself because you are in for the ultimate spiritual transformation! Then e-mail me at <u>Aku@blacksheepkickazz.com</u> because I would love to hear all about it. ☺

I've listed my lifestyle changes in the order that it occurred. Most of these lifestyle changes were introduced to me by Kevin Trudeau.

In his book *Natural Cures "They" Don't Want You to Know About*, my world was turned upside down as I learned and then found evidence of the ménage à trois between the government, FDA, and the pharmaceutical industry.

As you peruse the list, take note of how you feel at the thought of these lifestyle changes. Listen to the difference of what your BLACK SHEEP spirit is telling you and what the HERD is telling you. You can tell the difference by the way you feel. If you feel doubt, fear, frustration, or resentment, that is the HERD. If you feel joy, excitement, optimism, relief, hope, or motivation, then your BLACK SHEEP spirit is trying to tell you something!

I implemented the following 9 ACTION STEPS that helped clear the background noise in my mind, reducing my fear of the unknown:

1. *Invest in inspirational and motivational audios.*
2. *Turn off negative programs on the Tel-LIE-Vision.*
3. *Cook at home more often.*
4. *Journal success and gratitude.*
5. *The less mess, the less stress.*
6. *Exercise for thirty minutes at least three days a week.*
7. *Meditate at least fifteen minutes every day.*
8. *Start a new conversation.*
9. *Daily mantra: "I am no better than anyone else, and no one else is better than me!"*

1. **Invest in inspirational and motivational audios to listen to on your daily commute to and from work.**

    There are no words to describe how much of an impact listening to positive messages has had on my life. We are constantly judged and reminded of our "limitations." Only people like yourself who feel that their higher purpose in themselves invest in self-discovery material such as this guide. It's imperative that you continue to invest in maintaining a positive spirit; remember, when you **feel Good**, you **feel GOD**.

    The very first CD series I invested in was Les Brown's *It's Not Over Until You Win*. I listened to these CDs for two years every single day during my commute to and from work. I did not know that I was actually reprogramming my mind-set and changing my subconscious. I just fell in love with the way I felt when I listened to such a powerful message. I then alternated with Les Brown's CD series *The Millionaire in You*.

    If you feel you don't have enough time in your day, you absolutely have some time during your commute. You will soon experience less stress on your commute, and you will arrive at your job feeling renewed and equipped with a sense of purpose. When you feel a sense of **purpose**, you'll begin to have a different perspective at work, and the members of the shitty committee in your life will have minimal impact on your day. Listen to the audio of the BSKA Principles or other positive audios for twenty-one days and journal your feelings and experiences—what do you have to lose?

2. **Turn off negative programs on the Tel-LIE-Vision.**

    The very first thing Kevin Trudeau made me aware of is how much negative feedback I was receiving on a daily basis. I would watch the evening news with intrigue and fright as I intently listened to how close all of this violence was to my home! It made me feel afraid to go outside and very hesitant to help a fellow spirit in need. It unconsciously made me label and stereotype people based on their skin tone or environment. I even felt insecure about my own worth based on my skin tone and the area of Chicago I lived in.

It's disheartening to realize that all of this negative programming is purposely designed to keep you **feeling** bad. I decided to take a hiatus from the evening news. I felt relief after just **a few days**! I was no longer bombarded with the "murder and slasher" horror stories EVERY night that just so happen to air right before bedtime. Instead, I began watching the news program on public-access channels, which reported the news minus the violence.

> When there is no enemy within, the enemies outside cannot hurt you. (Winston Churchill)

After a while of a practicing a new habit, you become more sensitive and aware of new incoming information. I absolutely began to notice just how many negative television programs are aired at any moment of the day. Take a moment to flip the channels and notice how many crime shows, reality fight shows, negative news events, political warfare, and courtroom dramas you and your family are being inundated with on a daily basis.

It's been over ten years since I rid myself of cable TV altogether. I no longer feel unsafe in my own home, and I am not hesitant to help someone in need or talk to a stranger on the street. Don't get me wrong, I care about what happens in my community. I simply choose not to watch what a person disconnected from God can do to another person. I know that hurt people **hurt** people. I instead choose to serve my community by living my life with purpose as an example for others. I have never regretted canceling my cable. Since then, I feel so much lighter in my spirit—not to mention lighter in my wallet! Let's see, $100 per month over ten years saved me $12,000! WOW!

3. **Cook at home more often.**

It's no secret that processed foods are no good for your mind, body, or spirit. The chemicals and preservatives in these foods are a major cause of the growing health and disease epidemic in our country. It's certainly no easy task, but try to buy organic food replacements. According to several health and wellness Web sites, you should buy the following foods organic:

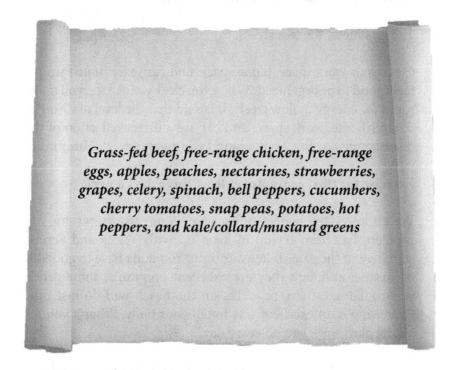

Grass-fed beef, free-range chicken, free-range eggs, apples, peaches, nectarines, strawberries, grapes, celery, spinach, bell peppers, cucumbers, cherry tomatoes, snap peas, potatoes, hot peppers, and kale/collard/mustard greens

I follow a Paleo diet (robbwolf.com) and still struggle to eat organic and cook at home, but I stick to an 80/20 rule. As long as I eat well 80 percent of the time and allow myself to eat whatever I want 20 percent of the time, I'm okay. So start small and please don't overwhelm or pressure yourself. Some change is better than no change at all. ☺

4. **Journal your success and gratitude**.

I've journaled off and on since elementary school. I would just write about the events of the day. But since learning about energy and spiritual law, I have learned how journaling can be used as a powerful tool for clarity and connection.

Journaling allows you to release the stress of the day onto paper. I later learned how to journal with intent. I will discuss journaling in more detail in Principle "P." Purchase a journal or notebook to keep track of all that you will attract into your life while expressing gratitude for all that you already have.

5. **The less mess, the less stress.**

Clear your work space, home space, and car space. It just simply **feels good** to be organized. When you clear your space, you make room for energy to flow freely. It is said that the level of disorder of your home, work space, and car are a direct reflection of the disorder of your life. Look around you right now . . . Hmmm . . .

6. **Exercise for thirty minutes at least three days a week.**

We all know the benefit of exercise—you can't go wrong. My problem has been trying to keep up with Venus and Serena starting out the gate. Take your time. You don't have to go P90X or Insane; although they are excellent programs, some gentle yoga, Pilates, tai chi, or walks on the beach will do just fine. Exercising is an excellent way to tell your body, "Thank you for all the hard work you do every day."

I meet up with my old coworkers and weight train for about two hours at least four days a week. I'm only able to do that because they hold me accountable. I've NEVER been able to stick to an exercise schedule for longer than a few weeks. I'm a Beachbody (beachbody.com) nut and bought a bunch of their programs but never finished one! My goal is to complete T25 by Shaun T. My point is, change isn't EASY for ANYBODY. It's the effort to be consistent whether you want to do it or not that wins the race! Finding the **right** partners or a personal trainer makes this change so much easier.

Try to do some form of exercise for thirty minutes at least three times a week. Switch it up so you don't get bored. Get it done in the morning; it's one less thing you have to think or stress about for the rest of the day. Then you'll **feel healthy**, you'll **feel Good**, you'll **feel God** about yourself. Notice a pattern here?

7. **Meditate at least fifteen minutes every day.**

I must admit, meditating was the hardest habit to implement on a daily basis. I just could not—no, I just *would* not find the time to meditate throughout my day. I just couldn't see the benefit. I was looking for immediate gratification, and sitting with my eyes closed just seemed pointless to me.

But ahh, . . . I caught myself feeling frustrated about meditating before I even gave it a try! I began to read more about meditation to understand why it is practiced by millions of people around the world. I started meditating, and I didn't notice a big difference and thought, "No big deal." It's when I STOPPED that I noticed the difference!

Meditation reduces stress, increases clarity of purpose, helps cure insomnia, lowers blood pressure, reduces road rage, improves memory, instills a peace of mind, allows self-acceptance, slows the aging process, builds self-confidence, improves relationships, increases productivity, and eliminates fatigue. The list goes on and on. It's FREE, and meditating requires no mats, tools, or equipment.

In the book *Ask and It Is Given*, Abraham-Hicks eloquently states,

> *An effective meditation distracts you from any physical awareness that causes resistance within your vibration, when you turn your attention away from what holds your vibration in a lower place, your vibration will naturally rise. Consciousness is withdrawn but while you are still awake. When you are asleep, you withdraw consciousness. But because you are asleep you are not consciously aware of what it FEELS like to be in that higher vibration. When you are awake and in that state of meditation, you can then consciously recognize what*

it FEELS like to be in that higher vibration. So in time
you will gain a new sensitivity to your vibration so that
you will immediately know whenever you are focusing
on something that is causing resistance.

In other words, meditating frees your mind and consciousness
of all the negative crap we feed it all day! When we meditate, we
are still awake, but our focus is on the silence that naturally raises
our emotional level from angry to peace—ahhh. Meditation
performed consistently trains your mind and consciousness to
react to events in our daily lives with patience and perspective
instead of an instant reaction instigated from the HERD.

So how do you meditate?

Well, let's clear up what meditation is NOT.

- You will not start out like a Buddha! I experienced thoughts
  swirling all around my head, which is how I noticed just how
  much mess I had to sift through. So don't worry, if the first
  few times feels chaotic, it takes practice.
- Chanting with "ohms" or "ahhs" isn't necessary. Chanting is
  merely a way to help you clear your mind by focusing on one
  thing, which is the chanting.
- You cannot have a "bad" meditation. Anytime you take the
  time to stop and relax your mind, it's a good thing.
- It doesn't matter what time of the day you meditate. Some say
  it's best in the morning to start your day. I tried to wake up
  in the morning and meditate, and it was beddy-bye-bye time
  all over again. Meditating in my car for thirty minutes after
  I leave the gym works best for me. I pop a meditation CD in
  then relax with no distractions.
- You don't have to meditate for hours at a time either. Try
  fifteen to thirty minutes, and you'll be fine. Set an alarm on
  your cell phone as a reminder to meditate.
- Please don't strain any muscles trying to sit like the
  kindergarteners. Preferably find a comfortable chair or
  anywhere that keeps your back straight. You may not want

to meditate while lying down . . . or it may be beddy-bye-bye time. ☺

Okay, now . . . how do you meditate?

Again, Abraham-Hicks describes this process so methodically, I feel like meditating right now. The following meditation process is from the book *Ask and It Is Given*:

> *Now, to begin the process of Meditation, sit in a quiet space where you are not likely to be interrupted. Wear comfortable clothing. It does not matter if you sit in a chair or on the floor, or even lie on your bed (unless you tend to fall asleep when doing so). The important thing is that your body be comfortable.*
>
> *Now close your eyes, relax, and breathe. Slowly draw air into your lungs, and then enjoy the comfortable release of that air (your personal comfort here is very important).*
>
> *As your mind wonders, gently release any thought, or at least do not encourage it by pondering it further— and refocus upon your breathing . . . As you quiet your mind, you may feel a sense of physical detachment. For example, you may feel no real difference between your toe and your nose. Sometimes you will feel the sensations of twitches or itches beneath your skin . . . once you have released resistance and soaring in your natural pure, high vibrations—you will experience various involuntary movement in your body. It may sway slightly . . . or you may yawn . . . all are indicators of a state of meditation.*

Try to meditate at least fifteen minutes a day. You'll soon notice that you'll look forward to that peace and quiet. Meditating ensures a reconnection to God, to your BLACK SHEEP spirit, on a daily basis.

You may ask, all of these benefits for taking time to breathe every day? ABSOLUTELY! Try it for twenty-one days and be sure to journal your thoughts and feelings about this time-tested spiritual practice!*

8. **Start a new conversation.** What I sorely missed during my time of transition was a consistent support group. I yearned to meet people that had similar drives and were on a mission to pursue their higher calling. The dissolution of the Master Mind group I created in 2011 left a gap I desperately needed to fill. I set my intention on finding a group of like-minded people that I can share my triumphs and pitfalls with openly and in confidence.

I asked God and left myself open to receive. In September of 2011, my prayers were answered in an e-mail I received from Christy Whitman inviting me to a teleseminar about becoming a Law of Attraction life coach! I didn't know how my life was about to change. The class was split into "pod" groups, and I was placed in a group among the most supportive, like-minded individuals that I had ever met in my life! There was an instant synergy we all experienced as we discovered that our experiences were closely related even though we were spread around the country!

We held each other accountable toward our progress, provided support for one another, brought topics to our calls that we feel our group could only understand. We laughed hard and we cried hard, holding each other's virtual hands every step of the way. There was no judgment based on the path you chose. No one looked down or thought different of me because of the choices I made in my life. We stayed focused on the days ahead, and we didn't dwell on mistakes of the past—a true friendship circle like no other.

How would it feel to be a part of a supportive group like this? What would it mean to you to escape the same negative conversations

---

* Included in the *BLACK SHEEP Kick-Azz Online Course Program* is the *BLACK SHEEP Kick-Azz Guided Meditation* download that will gently guide you through a peaceful spiritual journey of well-being. ☺

you encounter every day? What conversations are you having right now?

Are you discussing how much crime has gone up? What "trifling" thing one of the members of the shitty committee at your job has done? Who had the nerve to wear what outfit? How high your bills have gotten? Who paid the most to fill up their gas tank? Who slept with whose man on that reality show? How terrible your kids or your spouse are? What part of your body hurts today? What stupid thing has your boss asked you to do? How much weight do you need to lose or gain today? Take time to notice the type of conversations you have on a daily basis and the energy it carries with it.

Journal your thoughts.

Try introducing more positive conversations among your circle of friends. Each time, notice their reactions and responses. Do they sound hopeful, or do they shoot themselves in the foot before even getting started? I would love to know about your experience. Journal your thoughts and e-mail me at Aku@blacksheepkickazz.com

Having a circle of friends to hang out and party with is one thing, but having a circle of like-minded individuals to support you in attaining your wildest dreams and desires is absolutely PRICELESS!

Keep in mind that **you can be the one** that starts a different conversation with your friends. If the conversations surround the stress of work and the daily grind, direct your friends to get this guide. It will not serve them if they get a copy from you free. We all know people tend to take better care of things they actually pay for! Let them start to invest in the renewing of their own spirit—you are doing them a favor.

Remember . . . **YOU ARE NOT ALONE.**

9. **Daily mantra:** *"I am no better than anyone else and no one else is better than me!"*

Repeating this mantra before going into your work space will serve as a reminder that everyone has a story and is experiencing their lives based on their environments. One of the biggest lessons I've learned after working at all levels from temp to management is that regardless of the amount of our paychecks, we ALL go home and face the same types of stress from spouses, children, traffic, bills, and family.

Because of society's need to feel superior, personal problems of an entry-level or temp employee is not deemed as important as personal problems of managers. I worked at a company where the quality group worked seven days a week. Every person in the group was burned out from working so many hours and not seeing our families for MONTHS! During a meeting, the VP of the quality group that was well aware of our schedule made the comment that her family was going to be unhappy because she was going to be late THAT DAY flying home to see them.

Unfortunately, this mantra is rarely practiced by managers and supervisors. You must not allow their behavior to influence your outlook on others or the way you treat your coworkers. Release judgment of the shitty committee and simply choose to excuse yourself from their negative conversations.

1. What feelings have emerged as you read through the ACTION STEPS? What came up from your BLACK SHEEP spirit and the HERD?

_____

_____

_____

_____

_____

_____

_____

_____

_____

2. Which of the changes have you chosen to implement first in your daily activities and why?

_____

_____

_____

_____

_____

_____

PRINCIPLE "S"

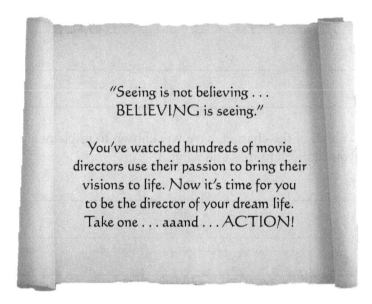

"Seeing is not believing . . .
BELIEVING is seeing."

You've watched hundreds of movie
directors use their passion to bring their
visions to life. Now it's time for you
to be the director of your dream life.
Take one . . . aaand . . . ACTION!

Scripting your dreams from a spirit of having already achieved it impresses upon your subconscious the reality of your desires. The benefit is the pure joy you feel as you write and let your imagination run wild with possibilities. Most people wait to "see" before they "believe," but only the successful few know they must "believe" their dreams are possible before they "see" results with their physical eyes.

The universe does not know the difference between what is real in your life and what you are imagining. **The universe only responds to how you feel about you**. So as you are describing your dream life, pay attention to your emotions. If you are describing living in Malibu in a house on the beach, you must accompany that vision with feelings of joy and excitement.

If you feel frustration and fear, it's because you are focused on "how am I gonna get it." You are not energetically aligned with your BLACK SHEEP spirit. As a reminder, you must also feel gratitude for where you are **right now**. So feel good about what you are writing with enthusiastic anticipation of God bringing it to you.

Use the following BLACK SHEEP Kick-Azz Dream Life as a starting point. It's important that you get comfortable, relax, turn on your favorite music, or sit in silence and let your imagination run wild!

Your BLACK SHEEP Kick-Azz Dream Life!

Imagine yourself waking up and it's five years in the future!

(Five years from today date: _____)

You are living your BLACK SHEEP Kick Azz Dream Life!! Describe where you are in great detail. What have you accomplished? Are you married or divorced? Describe your ideal mate. Describe your journey, the obstacles you overcame, and the person you've become because of them. Are you still at your current workplace? Describe your monetary achievement. What have you purchased? How is your passion serving you? Where have you traveled? Describe your relationships with family and friends. How do you feel? It's your story. Own it . . . Be proud . . . Go for it!

_____

_____

_____

_____

_____

_____

_____

Your BLACK SHEEP Vision Page

Now that you are floating at such a high energy level, let's keep the party going! The next two pages are another fun exercise to bring your BLACK SHEEP Kick-Azz Dreams to life! A Vision Page is a collage of pictures and images representing your dreams and desires. These images will raise your energy level and focus your conscious and subconscious on the achievement of your goals.

Have fun with this! Gather pictures and images from the Internet, magazines, newspapers, etc., that represent your BLACK SHEEP Kick-Azz Dream Life. Use a glue stick to paste these pictures and images on the next two pages.

For optimal effect, personalize the pictures. You will feel even more connected as you envision yourself living in the achievement of your goals and dreams. Spend a few minutes every day with these images and bask in the joy, freedom, and purpose that you feel. Vision pages are a great way to raise your energy level and align yourself with the achievement of your objectives.

For example, if your dream is to write a book, design the cover of the book and insert your name and photo on the cover as the author.

If your dream is to obtain a higher position in your company, create an image of a business card displaying your photo and the new job title.

If your dream is start your own business, add images of what the business will look like. Add pictures of people that have achieved success in your area of interest as inspiration.

BLACK SHEEP Vision Page 1

BLACK SHEEP Vision Page 2

PRINCIPLE "H"

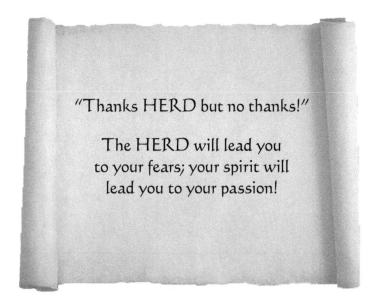

"Thanks HERD but no thanks!"

*The HERD will lead you
to your fears; your spirit will
lead you to your passion!*

Why Do So Few People Follow Their Bliss?

The no. 1 reason most people don't take the time to discover and pursue their passion is the fear of **JUDGMENT from other people**. The very thought of looking bad in front of others pressures most people to keep their passions and dreams dormant, oftentimes for a lifetime. They don't want to become the "talk of the day" among their family and friends. Most people live their lives doing everything possible to feel accepted by their parents, boss, coworkers, the church, family, and friends. There is a part of us that fears the unknown and would do anything to prevent change. There is a part of us that loves to follow the "norm" of society.

Judgment and fear of the unknown is what kept me at a job outside my passion for many years. A part of me kept saying, "You can't do anything else, you've been a chemist forever and that's all you've been trained to do." I kept hearing, "You don't have a passion and you don't have a clue where to find it, so get back to filling those beakers." I only **felt** that I was meant to be more than a chemist working a rotating shift. For years, I woke up every morning miserable thinking that this may be the routine of my life—talk about stressed!

What Is the "HERD?"

Over the last thirteen years, I've been obsessed with personal development and spiritual laws. Each of us were born with a unique divine purpose to be the best of who we were meant to be, which I've coined our BLACK SHEEP Spirit. In our spiritual universe, there exists a "group" of psychological elements whose goal is to keep us from changing who we are for fear of being harmed. I call this group of elements the "HERD," also known as the **EGO. The HERD encompasses the shitty committee in your life, your ego, your past experiences, your fear of judgment, your fear of failure, your fear of success, low self-esteem, and low self-worth**. The HERD can consciously and subconsciously supersede our higher calling. The HERD is **NOT** an outside entity that tempts us into misdeeds. The HERD is genetically a part of each one of us, and its main goal is to keep us safe from harm.

The HERD is our "**false** self." The HERD looks like you, walks like you, and talks like you. In most people, the HERD has been eating its Wheaties for many years and has now become bigger and stronger than your BLACK SHEEP spirit, our Divine Self. The HERD sees the world through your **physical eyes only**. Therefore, the HERD cannot look within itself for a higher purpose. From the day you were born, the HERD has been collecting and storing information of what other people have told you, the negative information from the tel-lie-vision and your past experiences and feedback from trying new things.

The HERD loves categories. The HERD loves to pass judgment and determine the worth of everyone it encounters: Are they rich or poor? Do they live on this side or that side of town? Are they educated or not educated enough? What is their ethnicity or race? Are they Catholic or Baptist? Are they married or divorced? Is their family rich or poor? The HERD can't wait to size someone up to compare and determine whether this person has more worth or less worth. The HERD treats that person accordingly, either with jealousy, discrimination, or with some other superficial behavior.

The HERD does not understand that one's circumstances could ALWAYS be better or worse, doesn't matter who you are, so why judge?

The HERD tells us that who we are is what we do and what we have. The HERD convinces us that the more stuff we have and the more "alphabet soup" we have behind our name, the better we are compared to other people. As a result, we become prisoners of our stuff and our job titles, and our sole mission in life is just to get more stuff! This is why so many people find it difficult to pursue their dreams. The HERD has convinced them that if you change course or dare to take a risk, you may very well lose all this stuff! Remember, the HERD has no higher calling, so who would it be without the job titles and all this stuff?! The HERD holds on especially tight and is extremely protective about its money, possessions and reputation. Now you understand why only 1 percent of the population controls over half of the country's wealth. They hold on to their wealth tighter than a pair of Spanx!

What Are Some of the Disguises of the "HERD"?

When I first sought out to pursue my passion, I had no idea what I was looking for. I just knew I liked to trade stock and options online, and I knew I loved to teach and train other people. Naturally, I figured I would teach and train other people to trade stocks and options. For some reason, this didn't feel good enough. I felt that my passion should be grander; I felt that I didn't know enough about trading to teach anyone else. I'd proposed a trading program to a networking group that wasn't accepted, and I never looked back. I wanted to feel like my passion was as lucrative as my last job.

I later realized that all that negative chatter was one of the many disguises of the HERD. The HERD was telling me to quit trying and go back to work to suffer and complain like everyone else. The HERD's reputation is its no. 1 priority. This is what the HERD may sound like:

- "I don't have time for this."
- "I'm not smart enough to create a product."
- "What if I fail? What would people think?"
- "I'm not pursuing that, it won't make enough money."
- "My spouse will leave me."

The HERD convinces you that you have the right to tell other people how to live their lives. The very issues the HERD has with others are a direct reflection of the insecurities the HERD has within itself. This is what the HERD sounds like toward other people:

- "I can't believe she's trying yet another business."
- "I won't buy a thing from her . . . She won't succeed with my support."
- "I can't believe she's still with him, I have lost respect for her."
- "I can't believe what she's wearing!"
- "She shouldn't wear her hair like that."
- "She's crazy for quitting her high-paying job!"

The HERD convinces us that we are right and everyone else is wrong. The HERD expects the world to revolve around its happiness. The HERD does not hold itself accountable for its own actions. Does this sound familiar?

- "Why is everyone driving so damn slow? Don't they know I'm in a hurry?!"
- "Can this sales clerk take any longer?"
- "I would have finished on time if my coworker didn't talk so much!"

Can You Tame the HERD?

The answer is absolutely YES! Thank God for our ability to become aware of our **feelings** and make a choice to change our thoughts.☺ You are the **shepherd** of **the HERD**, and your BLACK SHEEP spirit can step up and stand out!

The BLACK SHEEP within you regularly tries to communicate your purpose to you. It takes effort and courage to listen, feel, and hear our BLACK SHEEP over the voices of **the HERD**. It's very easy to side with the HERD because most of society lives by the HERD's rules.

The HERD tells you that you are separate from God, so you are separate from Good, Well-Being, Pure Love, and All-Giving. So this would also mean that you are separate from your purpose, your dreams and your desires. If God is ONE SOURCE that created you and all things including that beach house and that dream car, how can you be separate from them?

Your BLACK SHEEP knows that you are connected to every dream, passion, and desire you can imagine. You only need to align yourself with those desires using emotional guidance and not allow the HERD to talk you out of it.

Your BLACK SHEEP is always trying to guide you to your higher purpose. When you discover and pursue your passion, the **enthusiasm and inspiration** you **feel** is your BLACK SHEEP, your Divine Self, communicating to you that you are on purpose. Once you begin to listen and allow yourself to be guided, the disguises of the HERD become apparent. You will immediately identify the HERD's voice by the way you feel. Once identified, you can then say, "Thanks for your feedback, but no thanks!" Eventually, after continuously responding and rejecting the voices of the HERD, the fear of judgment will slowly minimize and will no longer have an impact on your pursuit to greatness.

Please keep in mind that this is not some new religious belief or cult; it's simply the result of my spiritual journey and what I have discovered about myself and observed in others. I've simply put one label on all the resistance I've had to overcome as I made the decision to transition from my job. No matter what you call it in bite-size pieces, its effect on your path to greatness is all the same. I AM an extension of God, of Good, of Well-Being and All-Giving. So I embrace my BLACK SHEEP, my unique Divine Self, my higher purpose, and I will believe in the BLACK SHEEP in you until your belief kicks in!

So who do YOU listen to?

Principle "H" Reflection

1. What disguises of the HERD have you identified in your life?

_____

_____

_____

_____

_____

2. What ways has your BLACK SHEEP spirit been trying to communicate to you?

_____

_____

_____

_____

_____

3. What can you do to reconnect with your BLACK SHEEP?

_____

_____

_____

_____

_____

4. How do you feel about reconnecting with your BLACK SHEEP?

_____

_____

_____

_____

_____

PRINCIPLE "E¹"

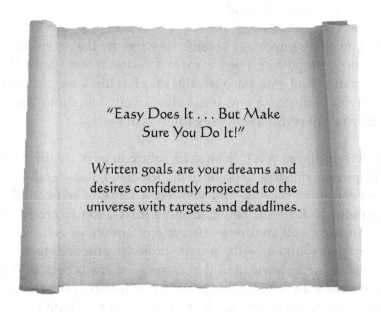

"Easy Does It . . . But Make
Sure You Do It!"

Written goals are your dreams and
desires confidently projected to the
universe with targets and deadlines.

Why Is Goal Setting Important?

Take a moment to look around your environment. Everything your eyes rest upon is the result of someone's goal. From the clothes you're wearing to the company you work for to the makers of the pen you are using to write, all originated from a thought and an executed goal.

When you set a goal in your mind, that means you have sensed dissatisfaction with where you are. This desire to achieve more is a way your BLACK SHEEP spirit signals to you your higher calling. You set a goal when you have identified a gap between where you are and where you want to be. It is within this gap that the magic happens. It is within this gap that you discover your potential by stepping out of your comfort zone and facing the voices of the HERD.

As you write your goals, the joyful and ambitious feelings of completing those goals are projected into the universe. The universe will begin to orchestrate the resources necessary to manifest those goals into the physical world.

Setting goals are important because they remove the overwhelming feeling of accomplishing big dreams and desires at first glance. If you have a goal to find your purpose, this may feel like a large endeavor. But as you brainstorm and break down your ideas into bite-size pieces, you will reveal a less-stressful path to success.

Goal setting allows you to plan your future in advance. By writing out inspired actionable steps, once implemented, your results create a momentum of success, and you feel a sense of self-confidence to continue to the end. You gain more inspiration to create more goals; in turn, you continue this cycle of ambitious achievement, self-confidence, and growth. You are projecting the feeling of "YES I CAN!" to the universe, and the universe by law is responding to your desires with "YES YOU CAN!" by manifesting the resources, circumstances, and people necessary to bring your goals into fruition!

As a wonderful bonus, you will no longer care about the opinions of the HERD. Only the focus on the achievement of YOUR goals will matter. ☺

My Goal-Setting Mistakes

I can admit for years I'd taken goal setting for granted. Every year, I would purchase a different type of sophisticated planner of various sizes. I loved to get the big ones with all the extra pages, and my eyes would light up with excitement as I thought about "finally" setting and achieving my goals for the year. The more pages that planner had, the better! Then every year, six months later, I'd look back and notice that I barely used the calendar or planner for all of its "sophisticated" purposes and I was now just keeping track of birthdays and bills due. Why?

I identified my mistakes while listening to goal-setting workshops of my virtual friends Bob Proctor and Tony Robbins. Their goal-setting workshops really uncovered where I was selling myself short when planning my goals. I've listed several mistakes I made below while setting goals to become a wealthy stock trader and a trainer to teach children about the stock market:

First, I wrote down a list of goals I wanted to accomplish that year. I felt confident perusing the list, and I was excited that **I finally wrote something down**! I was so excited because I finally felt I was taking action! The very first mistake I realized was that **I did not write the "WHY"** next to those goals. Writing down the "WHY," we need to achieve these goals to act as motivational reminders of the importance of succeeding.

The "WHY" *in my head* was obvious: "Duh, I want to make money." But simply making money did not entice a big enough motivation to raise my energy level high enough to take consistent, inspired action steps. I didn't connect my higher calling to teach by serving humanity. At the time, my dismal bank account balance changed my focus. But simply making money did not resonate with my Divine Self. Making money wasn't an important enough goal to keep me motivated and empowered to face the HERD.

Next, I discovered that the **image of my goal was not clear and concise**. I knew I wanted to make a profit of $100,000 in one year. I wrote it down and was excited about the amount, but I did not create a clear picture of what earning that amount of money would look like in my life. It didn't feel REAL in my subconscious as having already achieved it.

Why didn't it feel REAL? Well, upon looking further into my intent, I realized that the **goal was not my own**. At the time I set those goals, I had one thing on my mind—MONEY! I chose those goals to get the fast approval of other people just to show them I hadn't missed a beat when I left Corporate America. I did not feel connected to the process or the outcome.

Suffice it to say, I had **not developed a passion** to pursue and achieve my goals. The goals I set did not create a "burning desire" in me, which is essential to maintain the motivation to accomplish each task. I loved to trade stock and options, but it was **more of a *hobby* than my purpose.**

My goal to teach trading to children made me feel good on the level of serving humanity (which is my ultimate purpose in life). But the image in my mind of actually going to different schools to teach and tackling the public school system **did not feel good.** The goal of making $100,000 from trading felt great on an income level, but dealing with Uncle Sam, forming a trading business, and the process of registering a corporate structure **did not feel good.**

My goals were **not aligned with my spiritual values.** It's no wonder they went untouched. I was the only active trader I knew at the time. I had **not sought out the support of like-minded individuals that would hold me accountable** for my progress. I think we all can relate to how easy it is to say "I quit" to the man or woman you see in the mirror. It's not so easy to give up trying in a group that is undergoing the same challenges.

Lastly, I felt embarrassed because after six months, I still had not started much toward completing my tasks. **I felt bad for changing my mind.** I fell into the Herd's spell of believing that I only had one shot at this dream thing. I gave up on myself simply because I felt like if these goals didn't work, nothing would—that ideology couldn't be further from the truth.

Did any of my mistakes resonate with you? If so, what resonated with you and how does it make you feel?

_____

_____

_____

_____

_____

Set BLACK SHEEP Kick-Azz Goals in twelve steps!

1. *Decide what you want and write it down.* For the purposes of this guide, options may include deciding you want to discover your purpose or deciding that you want to transition from your current job and pursue your passion. **Make sure your goals are your own** and are not to seek the approval of other people.
2. *Decide and write down WHY you want it.* Your "why" must be aligned with your spiritual beliefs and values; just writing "money" may not cause a large enough surge of excitement and motivation to sustain your pursuit. Is it that you want to live a life of freedom? Are you tired of your daily stressful commute? Do you want to wake up excited with a sense of purpose? Do you want to travel the world with no time constraints? Are you tired of missing your children's school events? Do you want a schedule that will allow you more quality time with your family? Review your "Clarity" list and "Desire Statement" in Principle "C." Your "why" should resonate with your divine purpose.
3. *Create a detailed image of your goals completed.* Imagine what your life looks like now that you have achieved your goals. Once you have a clear image, write it down including as many details as possible. Describe in **present tense** the way you feel about yourself and how grateful you are for your blessings RIGHT NOW. Your subconscious doesn't know the difference between what is in the physical world and what is imagined. Your subconscious only responds to the way you **feel about you.**
4. *You must have a passion for your goals.* You will know you are on purpose based on your emotional guidance system. You will **feel good** and you will accomplish your tasks with joy, enthusiasm, and excitement. Keep in mind, it is only natural to experience dips in your enthusiasm, which is the reason your "WHY" must be significant enough to recharge your energy and motivation.
5. *Prepare for the disguises of the HERD.* The HERD loves to worry about the "how." **The "how" is none of your business.** When you focus on the "how," you are sending a signal of doubt to the universe. You are asking your **brain** for physical proof of your **divine** purpose. The HERD will surely answer you with "There's

no way you can do this because . . ." or "This is not for people like you, give up!"

6. *Meditate over your "WHY" statements for fifteen minutes.* Sit in silence and think about the impact on your family and your life once you achieve your goals. Now while you are in an elevated energy level, begin to **write down twenty to thirty <u>inspired</u> action steps** to achieve your goal.

7. *Number the inspired action steps by priority.* Number from 1 as most important to 20–30 as least important.

8. *Assign target dates for each action step.* Target dates induces a feeling of pressure on your conscious mind. This is a good pressure that will inspire consistent action and create momentum to accomplish your dreams and desires.

9. *Begin with task no. 1 and start immediately!* Complete one task at a time to prevent feeling overwhelmed.

10. *Find a buddy or supportive group to hold yourself accountable.* The *BLACK SHEEP KICK AZZ Online Course Program* teaches goal setting in more detail and is comprised of like-minded individuals just like you who are ready to pursue their passion in a safe and supportive environment conducive for spiritual growth and ultimate success! Go to blacksheepkickazz.com for more information!

11. *Track your progress by recording the actual completion dates.* It's okay if you change your task order, add tasks, or remove tasks. IT'S YOUR PLAN . . . **Feel good** with whatever adjustments you choose.

12. *Maintain a good attitude and don't quit!* Identify the HERD's disguises and immediately write them down. Then replace them with an affirmative statement from your BLACK SHEEP spirit and write it down. Trust yourself or trust in the positive feedback from your buddy or support group until your belief kicks back in. When your BLACK SHEEP spirit is aligned with your actions, your goals, dreams, and desires will be realized—IT IS LAW.

Principle "E¹" Reflection

1. What are your feelings around goal setting?

   _____

   _____

   _____

   _____

   _____

2. How do you feel about setting your goals using the twelve steps above?

   _____

   _____

   _____

   _____

   _____

3. What is the first goal you will set using the twelve BLACK SHEEP Kick-Azz goal-setting steps and why?

   _____

   _____

   _____

   _____

   _____

PRINCIPLE "E²"

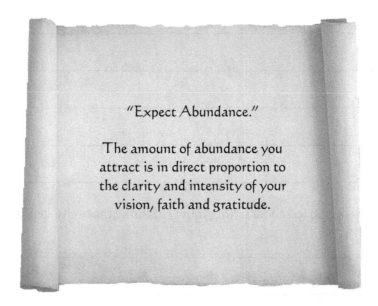

"Expect Abundance."

The amount of abundance you attract is in direct proportion to the clarity and intensity of your vision, faith and gratitude.

Although this workshop is about making a decision to stay or transition from your job from a place of power, the subject of money and energy could not be ignored.

We all were raised to have certain relationships with money. I was raised to see money as an elusive treasure. I thought of money as the Loch Ness Monster. People I didn't know saw it, but when I searched for it, I could never catch a glimpse! My experience has caused me to feel uncomfortable with large amounts of money. Every time I received a bonus check or tax refund, I would immediately find things to spend the money on until my checking account was back to a "comfortable" low balance. Since I never had access to millionaires, I subconsciously believed that I did not deserve large amounts of money.

One of the difficult parts of my transition of becoming an entrepreneur was the mental shift necessary to accept payments for my services.

It felt very uncomfortable to accept payment for work that I loved to do anyway. But it was perfectly okay to receive paychecks for work activities I despised!

Over the years, I spoke of money in terms of ambition. I wanted to make more of it; I recognized that when I didn't have enough, I assumed the harder I worked, the more I could earn, and I was always anxious to reach a certain salary so I could be happy, complete, and separate from those with less salaries.

So I raised my salary with every job position I accepted. But did I feel more abundant and happier? Ultimately . . . no. The more money I made, the more things I found to spend it on. There was always something I couldn't wait to buy with my next check. I went shopping for things to buy and spent money before I even received my check.

Any of this ringing a bell?

At **half** my salary, I found a way to live comfortably with less things, thinking if I just made more money, I would be set. Then I doubled my salary; after a while, I thought that if I just made more money, I would be set. What I experienced with money is the same as many people who live in a spiritual world called "**LACK**."

Are You Living in a Spiritual State of Lack?

Money, like everything else in the universe, is energy. You can attract more money or less money depending on the energy you project. At the time, my attitude was not gratitude of what I already earned. As I yearned for a higher salary throughout the years, I was actually telling the universe that what I had wasn't enough. I was in a spirit of lack. So when I obtained a higher salary, I found more things to purchase and felt dissatisfied with my higher salary. I was still in a spirit of lack.

In the book *Money and the Law of Attraction*, Abraham-Hicks states, "Any action that is taken from a place of lack is always

counterproductive, and it **always** leads to more of a feeling of lack."
Anyone in a state of lack cannot attract abundance.

You have a lack mentality if you have any of the following habits:

- Complain about not having enough money.
- Blame your spouse or children for your financial situation.
- Blame the government for your financial situation.
- Are jealous of your wealthy friends.
- Show judgment toward the way others spend their money.
- Gauge your worth and other people's worth based on their salary.
- Show resentment and anger when paying bills.
- Live a lifestyle above your financial means.

You Have a Right To Be "Rich Beyotch"!

Sorry, couldn't help it; I miss Dave Chappelle!

As I have purposely repeated many times over throughout this guide, you are an extension of God—Good, Pure Love, and All-Giving. It is your God-given right to be rich with an unlimited source of abundance, the same as your creator. Your financial situation has absolutely nothing to do with your job, spouse, children, etc. Your state of financial health has **everything** to do with your perspective about money. Remember, you create your own experiences and your own destiny.

How to Attract Abundance

The number no. 1 way to attract abundance into your life with lightning speed is to show gratitude while living through your BLACK SHEEP spirit! When you embrace the authentic side of you, your Divine Self, your BLACK SHEEP, you release negative resistance (the HERD) and allow all of God's blessing to flow effortlessly into your life. An "attitude of gratitude" aligns your spirit with the universe at the highest energy level. It is at this level that abundance is manifested into your experience.

When we speak of money, most people speak in terms of where they are right now and their lack of enough money. In order to raise our energy and become aligned with God, we must speak in terms of where we want to be as if we already possess this abundance. So in addition to being grateful and satisfied with what we have, we must also be grateful for the abundance that's coming as if it is already in our experience.

The "Dyann Effect"

One of my very close friends, Dyann, is by far the smartest woman I know. She leveraged her intellectual ability to climb the corporate ladder very quickly and in a short amount of time. She makes the habit of learning about EVERY ASPECT of her job and adds value to herself, thus positioning herself to qualify for available promotions and opportunities.

The "Dyann Effect" is simple— *learn more about your job!* The HERD discourages this by telling you, "Your company doesn't appreciate you" or "Why bother, they play favorites when promoting." But serving more aligns you with God, which is All-Giving, Pure Love, and an unlimited source of abundance. For those of you who are working full-time and may desire to advance in your company, yes, doing more than what you are paid for aligns your spirit with abundance. Find a way to *serve more*. Since you are more than likely experiencing "organizational" burnout symptoms, **find a *solution* to a problem that bugs you and leverage this unique knowledge to advance in your company.**

Dyann influenced me to learn about departments outside of my own that resulted in my promotion to project manager at a major pharmaceutical company. I was not a certified project manager nor did I take any specialized training. My knowledge of the various departments in my company along with a pleasing personality proved sufficient for advancing in my career—and it wasn't even my passion.

You must become the "go to" person, and more importantly, you *must* maintain a good attitude and learn more from a feeling of PURPOSE. As a result, you can very quickly begin to attract abundance into your life via promotions, bonuses, and job security.

Below are some other ways to help release resistance to allow abundance:

- Create a clear vision of what you want with more money, why you want it, and how you would feel about yourself.
- Avoid occupying your mind space with articles, TV programs, or books showing pictures of poverty or sick and abused children. You can do so much more to assist in these areas when you attract abundance yourself and teach others in poverty to do the same. Simply giving more money doesn't solve the problem as we can attest in our own lives. We must teach a new way of thinking. We must switch from a poverty mind-set to one of abundance.
- Read magazines and TV programs that will aid in visualizing the life that you desire.
- Speak of your financial situation from a spirit of abundance. Instead of saying "I'm sick of being broke!" say "I know I will have what I need when I need it—I'm created from abundance!"
- Thank God as you pay your bills. God has blessed you with the abundance to pay for the services you require to live a comfortable life.
- You and only you made the decisions that resulted in your financial situation. The quicker you stop blaming others and hold yourself accountable, the quicker you release the resistance that prevents the flow of abundance into your life.
- God is an unlimited source of abundance; there is enough for everybody. There is no point to feel jealousy or insecurity toward other people's wealth.

In *The Science of Getting Rich*, Wallace D. Wattles proclaims,

> *To think health when surrounded by the appearance*
> *of disease or think riches when in the midst of the*
> *appearance of poverty requires power, but whoever*
> *acquires this power becomes a master mind.*

Principle "E²" Reflection

1. Describe your feelings and the relationship you have with money right now.

_____

_____

_____

_____

2. What negative and limiting thoughts or statements did you identify?

_____

_____

_____

_____

3. Replace these negative statements with affirmative statements.

_____

_____

_____

_____

_____

4. As a spiritual being with unlimited abundance, **tell a new story**
    using your new affirmative statements. Sentences may begin with
    "Thank you, God, now that . . .," "I feel blessed because . . .," "I am
    in the process of . . ."

_____

_____

_____

_____

_____

_____

_____

_____

_____

PRINCIPLE "P"

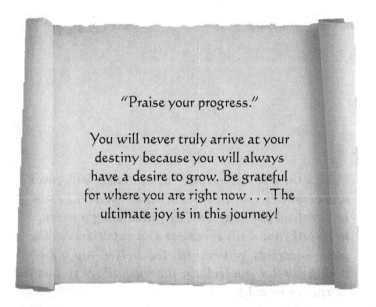

"Praise your progress."

You will never truly arrive at your destiny because you will always have a desire to grow. Be grateful for where you are right now . . . The ultimate joy is in this journey!

Life is a journey. We will never reach a point when we stop wanting and desiring for something more or something better. Our constant wanting is how our universe originated, and it's what keeps it expanding. This workshop is designed to empower you to live your purpose NOW. You possess unique talents and abilities that need only to be tapped and allowed to be released. It is within this BLACK SHEEP spirit that true happiness resides. It is calling itself forth through each symptom of burnout you experience.

The moment I stopped allowing the HERD to run my life and I began to listen to my BLACK SHEEP, I have since experienced a life of pure joy, happiness, purpose, and freedom. Life became fun and exciting as I used my emotional guidance to guide me to achieve my dreams and desires. I notice the HERD in my life immediately, and I quickly replace any "stinkin' thinkin'" with thoughts of Good, God, Pure Love, my BLACK SHEEP!

Review these principles on a regular basis to discover and empower your BLACK SHEEP. Then make sure to "Praise Your Progress" by purchasing a journal to record your daily successes and experiences. The more successes you record, the better you'll feel; and the better you feel, the more successes you will attract in your life.

All you need now is a support system of like-minded individuals to hold you accountable for your success. Congratulate yourself!!! You've come this far, which is further than most people. Let's end this workshop on a high energy level!

Principle "P" Reflection

1. What ten things are you grateful for in your life?

_____

_____

_____

_____

_____

_____

_____

_____

_____

2. What ten things do you **appreciate** about your job?

_____

_____

_____

_____

_____

_____

_____

_____

_____

3. Who else and what else in your life will be positively impacted by living through your BLACK SHEEP spirit and achieving your dream?

_____

_____

_____

_____

_____

4. How will you use the information you learned in this guide as a tool to grow?

_____

_____

_____

_____

_____

5. What decision have you come to regarding a decision to stay or transition from your job? Why have you come to this decision?

_____

_____

_____

_____

_____

6. What are your next five inspired action steps?

_____

_____

_____

_____

_____

Congratulations!! You Kicked Azz!!

Please take the time right now to take a deep breath and give yourself a pat on the back!

By completing the exercises, you've achievedthe following:

- You are now aware that you are blessed with a unique BLACK SHEEP spirit and have made the commitment to discover and pursue your passion!
- You've created a spiritual drive by writing a compelling life-purpose statement in great detail based on your strengths and imagination.
- You feel at peace from learning to be okay with where you are. You've learned to hold yourself accountable and to forgive yourself and others.
- You created a Kick-Azz desire statement that should be read daily by identifying what you DO want right now based on what you DON'T want.
- You've learned how to hear your higher calling with nine ways to clear your environment and allow divine inspiration to flow into your consciousness.
- You've brought your passions to life through scripting and visioning exercises.
- You are now aware of some of the disguises of the HERD and how they can impact your motivation and success.
- You've learned how to set Kick-Azz goals in twelve steps and how to actually achieve them!
- You've explored your relationship with money and determined if you are in a spiritual state of lack.
- You've learned the need to be easy with your journey. You've praised your progress so far and understood that the joy of life is in the journey!

I created this guide as a spiritual personal development starter kit. I've always felt deep in my soul that life was meant to be joyful and fun. If you are not spiritually and mentally prepared, bad bosses, shitty coworkers and non-supportive friends and family can rob you of that joy then you may end up questioning your purpose.

We dreamers know that we can not share our journaled answers with just anybody. God has blessed us with the ability to think outside the box and we should not take these inspired gifts for granted. We must clarify and protect them.

So how do you sustain your new found passion and purpose? Without question the first step to continue fortifying your mind and spirit is to connect with supportive like-minded people who are determined to finally create pathways to bring their dreams to fruition.

The second step is to always dive deeper to understand and build confidence about who you are. Ongoing personal development training will continue to solidify your spiritual foundation and provide you with insight and questions that will further empower your purpose.

I invite you to join a movement of people who are proud to be BLACK SHEEP stepping up and standing out to discover, protect and pursue their passions. Go to blacksheepkickazz.com to join the movement and enroll in the BLACK SHEEP Kick Azz Online Course Program.

You've started on the path to bliss. The HERD will tell you this guide is enough, your BLACK SHEEP spirit knows the party has just begun :) Join and enroll today!

NOTES

ABOUT THE AUTHOR

Aku Esther Oparah is an author, speaker, ICF-certified life coach, and corporate trainer. Aku earned a bachelor's of science degree in chemistry and worked fifteen-plus years as a chemist, supervisor, project manager, and lead auditor at various companies.

After experiencing a panic attack from job burnout, Aku decided to leave Corporate America and pursue her dream to become an entrepreneur. Aku always felt deep down that she was meant to be more than her job titles. Through divine inspiration, she discovered that her passion was to teach and empower others who also felt like square pegs being pounded into round holes. Her greatest fear is living a life full of regrets.

After ten-plus years of studying spiritual personal development, Aku founded the BLACK SHEEP Kick-Azz Movement. Aku created this environment to serve as the spiritual pulse of a movement of people that are burned out in their careers and are ready to discover, protect, and pursue their passions. Aku created the *BLACK SHEEP Kick-Azz Online Course Program* to spiritually empower and celebrate our unique God-given passions without fear of judgment from ourselves or from other people.

Aku lives in Chicago with her wonderful daughter Anaya. For more information about coaching services, online courses, or to hire Aku for speaking engagements, please visit BlackSheepKickAzz.com.

STEP UP AND STAND OUT BECAUSE BLACK SHEEP KICK AZZ!

Printed in the United States
By Bookmasters